Pers

Discipline

Using Power Messages and Suggestions to Influence Children Toward Positive Behavior

Carmen Y. Reyes

License Notes

This book is intended for personal and professional enrichment. You may not reproduce this book, except for teaching purposes. Duplicating this book for commercial use is not allowed. Thank you for respecting the hard work of this author.

SolidRock Press

Contents

Introduction

Language and communication are the keys in persuasive discipline. A core principle in persuasive communication is that the specific *language patterns* (words and phrases) a teacher or parent uses when disciplining children influence behavior. When teachers and parents control the messages sent to children, we control the way children feel and think about our messages, and when we control the way children feel and think about our messages, we are in control of their behavior. Carefully chosen words and crafted messages can actively create the mental images and mood needed in children to move them away from noncompliance and oppositional behavior and closer to comply with what they were asked to do. Simply put, persuasive discipline is *redirecting behavior through language,* using *influence* instead of power and dominance. Good persuaders are able to communicate with children using just the right words to get a positive outcome. Persuasive discipline contains enhanced language patterns and ways of talking that shift the emotional state of a child, influencing and promoting positive behavior.

Persuasion Techniques

Persuasion Technique 1: Assume that What You Want is True

If you talk and act as if what you want is true, your child will believe you. With a *positive assumption*, we take for granted that the child wants to do what we are asking; for example, asking, "Do you want carrots or celery?" positively assumes that the child wants and will eat one of these two vegetables.

Persuasion Technique 2: Use Positive Directions

When we use positive directions, we get higher compliance than when we use negative directions. Negative directions tell children what not to do; "Don't make noises," or "Don't hit your little brother" are examples of negative directions. On the other hand, positive directions tell children what they need to do to comply. Work in changing the negative directions you give children into positive directions. Shapiro (1994) recommends writing down the negative directions we typically say in one column, and then, in a second column, we change those statements into directions that tell the child, in a very specific way, what he or she should be doing instead. Always describe what you want in positive terms; for example, "Talk in a quiet voice" rather than "Stop shouting."

Persuasion Technique 3: Point Out an Acceptable Alternative

Positive directions guide the child toward a more appropriate behavior or alternative. Shapiro provides the following examples, "Making noises at the table disturbs other people during dinner. If you need to make noises, you can excuse yourself from the table and *go outside* for five minutes," and "When you hit your little brother you will have to go to time-out. *Try hitting this pillow* when you are angry." The phrases in italics are the acceptable alternatives. According to Schaefer (1994), when we point out an acceptable alternative, the child will be more likely to change the inappropriate behavior because he knows what he should do in addition to what to stop doing.

Persuasion Technique 4: Use More "Start" Messages and Fewer "Stop" Messages

It is easier to start doing something than to stop doing something, especially if the child is enjoying what she is doing. Apply this knowledge when disciplining children: instead of focusing the child on what to stop doing, focus her on *what to start doing*. For example, you can turn a "stop" statement like, "*Stop* wasting time!" into a *directive statement* such as, "Please, *return to your seat* and *get your reading book*." A teacher or parent skilled in persuasive discipline is able to suggest alternative ways of behaving rather than constantly saying "No," "Don't," or "Stop that."

Persuasion Technique 5: Replace the Word "Start" with the Word "Continue"

It is even easier to continue doing an activity that is already in progress than to start doing something new. You will find less resistance to requests and commands by just dropping the word "continue" in the sentence. For example, saying, "Justin, *continue* doing your homework" or "Justin, *continue* reading your book."

Persuasion Technique 6: State Rules Impersonally

For example, you can say, "*The rule in this class* is no wearing caps in the classroom," or "*The rule in this house* is no pushing your sister." Avoid taking ownership of the rule saying things like, "I want…" or "I expect to see that you…" The beauty in using *impersonal wording* is that puts the child in conflict with an impersonal rule; the child and the adult are not in conflict, neither the child with another student (Schaefer, 1994).

Persuasion Technique 7: Give Alpha Commands

A command is a short authoritative statement that demands instant compliance. Walker and Walker (1991) identify two types of commands:

1. *Beta commands* involve vague and multiple directives, given simultaneously, and they do not provide a clear criterion for compliance. With a beta command, we do not give the child adequate time and opportunity to comply; in other words, when we give a beta command, we do not tell the child exactly what he needs to do to comply. Beta commands are usually accompanied by excessive verbalizations. Walker and Walker present the following example of a beta command, "Jimmy, your room is always such a mess! Why don't you *clean it up* instead of waiting for me to do it for you? I'm so tired of always picking up after you!" The phrase in italics is the beta command; everything else is just venting. Most importantly, the directive given is so ambiguous that it is going to be

difficult for Jimmy to comply with what the parent wants.

2. *Alpha commands* involve a clear, direct, and specific statement without additional verbalizations. Alpha commands allow a reasonable period of five to fifteen seconds for the child to respond. They are short (around ten words) and tell the child exactly what to do; for example, "Jimmy, pick up all the toys from the floor and put them on the shelf."

Beta commands lower the rate of compliance; alpha commands increase compliance. However, both types of commands can escalate into a demand, which is why we should use commands carefully and only if they are necessary to the situation. To give alpha commands, Walker and Walker (1991) recommend:

- Use positive, descriptive terms.

- Give only one command at a time, followed with a period to comply.

- Do not argue with the child, and do not reissue the command or give a different command to the child.

- If the child does not comply, repeat the same command, beginning with, "You need to…" and giving a mild consequence.

- If the child complies, give her positive attention and *descriptive praise*, e.g., "Good, you responded promptly to what I asked you to do." We get better results when we move closer to the child to give the command *(close proximity technique)*.

Persuasion Technique 8: Give More Requests and Fewer Commands

Do not give a command if a request would do it as well. Always use more requests and suggestions than commands or direct orders. Unlike a command, a request carries no pressure to comply, implying that *the child has a choice*; more specifically, we are giving the child the opportunity to either accept or refuse the request. We state requests in the form of questions accompanied by social conventions such as "Would you please…?" or "I would like you to…" (Walker and Walker, 1991). In other words, a request is asking; a command is telling. As with commands, you will get better results, if you (Schaefer, 1994):

1. Stay close to the child, rather than making your request from a distance.

2. Make eye contact.

3. Limit yourself to two requests, making the same request only twice, and avoiding making different requests at the same time.

4. Turn down your voice volume, using a soft but firm voice.

5. Use "start" requests rather than "stop" requests.

6. Give a reasonable time for the child to comply to your request (five to fifteen seconds).

7. Make a clear, descriptive request using positive wording; for example, "Please turn off the lights."

8. Reward compliance with a smile and a "Thank you."

Persuasion Technique 9: Give Choices to the Child

Providing opportunities to make choices is highly effective in increasing positive behavior and compliance in children. Try to give the child some freedom of choice; for example, "*Either* play quietly *or* go upstairs to play." According to Schaefer (1994), giving choices increases children's independence and decision-making skills.

Persuasion Technique 10: Use Forced Choices

To make sure that the child does the behavior we want, we can limit the choices given to only two. We call this technique *forced choices* or *double binds*, because, regardless of what the child chooses to do, she is still complying with the behavior that we want. An example of a forced choice is, "You have two choices: either go to bed right now so that *I can read you a story*, or you go to bed immediately after the TV show." Increase compliance to your favorite option by making it easier for the child to choose the option that you like best, while making it harder to select the less attractive choice. Similarly, make your preferred choice a more attractive and desirable option for the child. In the example, the parent raised the desirability of going to bed "right now" by including in this choice an activity that is valuable to the child: reading her a story. When there is more than two choices available, offer the option you want the child to take *first* or *last*, never in-between other choices. Some types of forced choices are:

1. *Revealing choices*; for example, "Do you want milk or orange juice with your lunch…and salad… carrots only or with green peas…? What fruit do you want, pear or apple?"

2. *Hierarchical choices*; for example, "Do you want the bigger ball or the smaller one?" "How many pages are you going to read before the break, five or ten?"

3. *The contrasting choice.* With this choice, you offer first something that has very little chance for the child to choose, making it sound as something inevitable. Then, you follow with the real

alternative; for example, "You can go to bed right now… or you can pick up your toys."

We can increase compliance to forced choices by helping the child feel that what she is doing is her own idea. You might say, "What would you rather do, wash the dishes or take out the garbage?" In the classroom, the teacher can ask something like, "When do you prefer to finish the math problems, after silent reading or after lunch?"

Persuasion Technique 11: Ask Leading Questions

Just presenting our main point in the form of a question, rather than as a declarative statement, is extremely influential. Each time we deliver the leading information in the form of a question, we avoid overwhelming and forcing the child, sending the message that it is the child's decision to make. However, we can enhance the persuasive power of questions by asking carefully crafted questions that influence the child in thinking in a particular way. Leading questions include either the answer or point we are trying to make, and they send the child in the direction that we want. When we ask leading questions, we eliminate all unwanted alternatives, moving the child in the direction of a specific alternative. Some examples of leading questions follow.

1. *Questions that make an assumption*; for example, asking, "How much your reading grade will go up this year?" assumes that the reading grade will go up this year. You are forcing the child into thinking first and foremost about the reading grade going up.

2. *Questions that link something that happened earlier, and it is still in the child's mind, with what you are suggesting now.* For example, "I was really disappointed when we yelled. How do you feel about talking quietly?"

3. *Questions that remind the child of previous agreement*; for example, "I'm glad that we agreed to talk about this situation. Can we also agree about talking quietly?"

4. *Questions that give two options, making one option more desirable*; for example, "Do you prefer reading

your book here or at the listening center, *which is quieter?*"

5. *Questions that link the past with the future (cause and effect),* e.g., "If you go to bed late, what will happen in your math test tomorrow?"

6. *Questions that lead the child into thinking of consequences or implications,* e.g., "If you keep getting into trouble each time you hang out with Eric, then what you think will happen the next time the two of you hang out? What happened the last time?"

7. *Questions that lead the child to agree with you.* You can accomplish this by saying only what you want the child to consider, without mentioning other possibilities; for example, "Do you agree that we need to discuss this issue?" and "Is it true that you are feeling more relaxed now that we talked?"

8. *Questions that lead the child into doing something for you.* For example, "Can you help me move these boxes to the garage?"

9. *Questions that lead the child to alternative behaviors*, e.g., "Would you be willing to consider_____?" "Do you mind doing _____ instead?" or "Would you prefer doing something else?"

10. *Questions designed to dissuade the child not to do something.* The trick here is making the child think that you are accepting the negative behavior, and then redirecting the child to an alternative behavior. For example, "I understand you might not want to stop hanging out with Eric, but will you?"

11. *Questions that prevent, or get the child not to do the behavior.* Do this by *refocusing* the child from the negative behavior to a positive alternative. For example, "Who else do you want to hang out with?"

Persuasion Technique 12: Manipulate the Size of the Request to Make it Look Smaller or Bigger

You have two ways of doing this:

1. *Breaking down your persuading* (from smaller to bigger). Smaller requests are easier to understand and to comply. With this technique, we move the child to make a larger commitment by asking for a smaller commitment first, e.g., asking the child to read only five pages of the book, and after he complies, asking him to finish reading the book. A variation of this technique is asking for something small first, and when the child complies, we ask for something bigger, and finally something even bigger. For example, read five pages, then read the next ten pages, and finally, finish reading the book.

2. *Making the bigger request first* (from bigger to smaller). This technique is the opposite of breaking down our persuading. Here, we make the biggest request first, something that the child may find

excessive and will likely refuse, and when the child refuses, we ask for something that requires less effort and feels more reasonable to the child; in other words, we get a "no" first so that we can get a "yes" last. For example, first, you ask the child to read the whole book, and then you reduce the request to reading *only* ten pages. This technique uses the *contrast principle*; by contrast, the second request seems smaller and easier to agree with when compared with the initial request.

Persuasion Technique 13: Buttering Up

Schaefer (1994) describes this technique as doing the child a favor in order to make him feel obligated to return the favor later on; that is; we reward the child in one area before expecting compliance in another area. For example, excusing the child from doing one of his daily chores, and then saying that in return you want him to study one hour longer.

Persuasion Technique 14: Use Pauses

We can add a pause before or after the key message, suggestion, or command in a sentence or a paragraph to enhance the persuasive power of the message. A pause before a key point increases tension and adds emphasis (e.g., "Would you please… *sit down*"). A pause after the key point lets the key point sink in (e.g., "*Please put the toy on my desk…* before lining up"). Pausing after giving the child a suggestion or command helps the suggestion or command sink in the child's mind.

Persuasion Technique 15: Visualizing

When you want the child to experience a particular emotion, simply get her to recall a time when she experienced the emotion. For example, if you are trying for a sad child to feel happy, or for an angry child to relax, get the child to *visualize* (to see in her mind) a time when she was happy (or relaxed). Positive *images* (thoughts) of happier and/or calmer times help bring on positive *feelings* of happiness and relaxation. In turn, these positive feelings (happiness or calmness) deflate the negative feelings (sadness or anger), pushing negativity out of the way. Imagining or picturing a different and more positive feeling helps the child shift into the emotional state that the mind is creating.

To facilitate shifting into this happier and calmer state, tell the child to remember a time when she experienced happiness or calmness; for example, during story time or a visit to the park. If the child has difficulty recalling, you can suggest a time and describe the experience. Then ask the child to tell what she is seeing in her mind and what happens next. Keep expanding the child's description to make the visualization more vivid. When the child recalls the happy or calm memory, the sensations associated with the memory act like suggestions that shift the child to a new mental state. The memory evokes the images, and the images evoke the new feeling; in other words, imagining how happy or calm she was then, makes her feel happier or calmer now. To strengthen this visualization, pause between images to give the child time to see the movie in her mind. When you pause, take notice and mention to the child the physical signs (facial expression and body language) that signal that the child is moving into the new state.

Persuasion Technique 16: Wondering

Wonder aloud about things you want the child to do, to believe, or to achieve. Wonder if the child can do it. Wonder about what might have happened or will happen. Wonder about the *benefits* for the child of doing it. Wonder if the child is already feeling _____ (e.g., calmed and relaxed). Say things like, "*I wonder* what will happen when you let go of that _____ (e.g., angry or self-defeating thought)."

Persuasion Technique 17: Use Odd Numbers

This is also known as the *pique technique*. When we include an odd number as part of the request, we are making an unusual request that leads to confusion and even wonder of why we are asking for something so peculiar. This extra second of confusion and wonder is what adds persuasive power to the request. For example, "Can you spare 19 cents?" rather than asking for a quarter. With children, for example, tell the child that the toys must be on the shelves at exactly 13 minutes after 2:00, or that you want the lights off and the child in bed exactly at 9:27. The child puts all her attention in the odd time, which distracts her from refusing.

Persuasion Technique 18: Linking

Link something you want with something the child wants; for example, "When you _____ (what you want) then you will get _____ (or this will happen) (what the child wants)." Link negative behavior with a consequence that the child does not want, e.g., "If you two keep talking, you will have less computer time." Link a low probability behavior with a strong probability behavior, making it clear that the path to the strong probability behavior is by complying with the low probability behavior (e.g., "After you finish the division problems, you can eat a snack").

Persuasive linking shows the child the path to what he wants, as well as which route to avoid.

Persuasion Technique 19: Use Repetition

Used wisely, repetition has a strong persuasive value. We can repeat key words or key phrases in our message. We can use the same words or the same phrases throughout the message, or we can use different words and phrases; what matters is that the key words or phrases carry the same meaning. There are three basic repetition techniques; the third one, the hammer, requires a more advanced level of language sophistication than the first two techniques.

1. *The triple technique* helps us emphasize the key message. The triple can be three single words, three phrases, or three complete sentences, but it must be three items that are related and that fit together to make an impact. The triple can be as simple as repeating the same item three times (e.g., the word "continue" or any other key word repeated three times), or as sophisticated as connecting three key

themes. For example, saying something like, *"And now that you are calmer, you feel ready to <u>pay attention to my words</u>, <u>think carefully about what happened,</u> and <u>tell me what other option you have to settle this problem</u>."* In this example, each key message in the triple is also a *hidden command* (Persuasion Technique 22). We can also connect three items in a sequence or three steps to reach a goal. To further connect the triple, we can change our vocal tone (rising or reducing pitch) when we mention each key item or step.

2. *The jackhammer technique* is mainly for use during an emergency to freeze and stop a risky behavior. With this technique, we repeat a single word or a short phrase three times and quickly. Steadily, we increase the volume of our voice; for example, "no! No! NO! DON'T HIT HIM! NO! NO!! NO!!!"

3. *The hammer technique* helps emphasize a key theme across a number of phrases and sentences. In the following example, the teacher gives directions to the class; pay attention to the message emphasized, "You will do the reading." With the right intonation,

the phrases underlined turn into *hidden commands* (Persuasion Technique 22).

You are going to read the first two chapters of your novel. You are expected to finish your reading in forty-five minutes or less. When you find a word that is hard to pronounce, or if you need the meaning of a new word, ask your reading partner for help; partners help partners stay focused and engaged. You must do the reading as silently as you can, so that we do not interrupt other readers, and remember to summarize the two chapters in your reading log.

Persuasion Technique 20: Use Power Sentences

When we use power sentences, we become more persuasive. Power sentences include at least one of the following elements:

1. Power sentences are *short* to make your point with a punch. You can use a phrase, or even a single word, as your whole sentence; for example, "Start now" or

"Quiet." With a short sentence, the child gets the whole meaning of the communication in one-step. A longer sentence blends in with the background noise and the child may miss the key message. A short sentence is easy to say, easy to remember, and easy to understand; three key elements in persuasive discipline.

2. Power sentences use *modal verbs*, e.g., can, may, could, should, and must. We use modal verbs to make something more or less important, depending on what we want to emphasize in the message. Examples of power sentences using modal verbs are:

   - To find the meaning of your new vocabulary words, you *can* work with your reading partner.

   - Here, you *could* fold these sheets.

   - If you want to finish faster, you *should* help each other.

   - You *must* clean this room in one hour.

3. To create interest, *divide the power sentence into two parts*, e.g., "Today we are going to do… (speech pause)… something really interesting!" A

divided sentence grabs children's attention because they want to know how the sentence is going to end (Nitsche, 2006).

4. To maximize persuasive power, *put the main impact at the end* of the sentence (final impact); for example, "You can go to the math center… *now.*"

Persuasion Technique 21: Use Power Paragraphs

A power paragraph includes some or all of the following elements:

1. *Few sentences.* In a power paragraph, do not use too many sentences; about three or four sentences are enough.

2. *Short sentences.* Use a short sentence at the start of the paragraph to grab the child's attention, and another short sentence at the end of the paragraph to summarize and identify the end of the message. Additionally, use short sentences to summarize after a long description or an explanation.

3. *Sensory language and pictorial descriptions.* When we paint pictures, sounds, and sensations with our words, we gain immediate attention and greater understanding, which by itself enhances the persuasive power of our message. Using sensory language triggers the child's senses, rather than having the child interpret the message cognitively (by analysis). In addition, once we use a pictorial description, we can create a solution using another picture, e.g., a brick wall (problem) can be scaled by a ladder (solution) (Mahony, 2003). A well-developed sensory message helps the child use all three main sensory modalities: (1) the visual modality by picturing the situation, (2) the auditory modality by talking about what is happening, and (3) the kinesthetic or tactile modality by stating how one is feeling.

4. *Power words.* For a greater impact, carefully place one or two power words in the message. Kinds of power words are:

   - *Identity or belonging words:* you, we, all, friends, team, everybody, together

- *Words that create interest and motivate:* love, favorite, interested or interesting, like, curious, discover, enjoy, fantastic, useful, good, challenge, important, wish, engaging

- *Agreement words:* yes, agree, consider, fair, settled, willing, compromise

- *Words that regulate behavior:* now, easy, quick, fast, simple, soon, brief or briefly

- *Words that inspire confidence and trust:* right, good, sure, certain, secure, guaranteed, confident, positive, reliable, strong

- *Safety words:* safe, protect, support, help

5. *Final impact.* To maximize the persuasive power of your paragraph or message, put the main point at the end; for example, "To solve the word problems you need to do _____ and _____."

Persuasion Technique 22: Use Hidden Commands

With this technique, we hide the command within the longer sentence; the other words in the sentence distract the child away from any resistance to the command. We emphasize our hidden command by *changing the tone of our voice*, more specifically, changing pitch when indicating the action (verb) that we want.

Types of hidden commands would be:

1. *The "I wonder" command;* for example, "I wonder if you could <u>organize your closet in 45 minutes</u>."

2. *The doubt command.* With this command, we sound uncertain that the child is able or willing to perform the action; for example, "Can you reach that top shelf? Great! Could you help me <u>put these boxes away</u>?"

3. *The assumption command;* here, we act and talk as if the child is going to obey the command. For example, "After you <u>organize your closet</u>, do you want a glass of milk?" "Here, <u>empty these grocery bags</u> and I will start fixing the dinner"; "Which end

of these sheets you will <u>fold</u>?" "How many <u>pages</u> are you going to <u>read</u> before lunch?"

Persuasion Technique 23: Use Suggestions

We make a suggestion when we guide the child to consider an idea or thought; for example, "You might want to consider this…" or "Maybe if you try it this way…" Schaefer (1994) identifies two main types of suggestions:

1. *Indirect suggestion;* for example, "From what I hear, you feel that the best way to settle this is to let Cindy know that she needs to ask you before she borrows your markers." An indirect suggestion simply strengthens an idea that is already present in the child's mind.

2. *Positive suggestion* is the act of attributing to the child a positive quality even when there is only minimal evidence that the child actually has the attribute or quality. We inspire the child to behave in a positive way by suggesting that he is already behaving that way to some degree. Some examples:

- You seem much stronger than you have ever been, so I know you are going to be very brave.

- Ricky and you are best friends, so I know you want to settle this issue with him.

- At heart, you are really an orderly child. You want to keep your things neat and orderly so that you can find them.

- You do not give up easily, so you are going to try hard and do your best.

Positive suggestions work best when the quality that we attribute to the child is not too discrepant from the child's character and ability; in other words, the child is able to perform the behavior or skill that we are attributing him. In the following example, the teacher is using positive suggestions to reduce the tantrum behavior in a kindergartener:

You are really getting bigger and bigger, and smarter and smarter every day. Soon you will be so very big that the tantrums will go away. Maybe it will be next week; perhaps you will be so big by tomorrow, or maybe the next day, that, when another child bothers you, you will say to yourself, 'No, I won't get mad. I'm not going to have a tantrum today because I'm a big girl now.' You just stay calm. Big girls do not have tantrums. That is just what little kids do. You say to yourself, 'I'm going to be a big girl,' and you stay out of trouble. Yes sweetheart, you are getting big and smart, and soon the tantrums will disappear... the tantrums will go away... just go away...

Persuasion Technique 24: Establish Rapport

The more children think you are a friend, the more they will like you and will be willing to listen to what you have to say. As a stranger, our influence is limited, but as a trusted friend, who knows how much more we can accomplish. Our persuasion is a lot easier when the child trusts and likes us. Gaining and maintaining rapport is the ability to elicit responses in the child. Like dancing partners, people in rapport mirror and match each other in posture and gesture (complementary body language). The key to rapport is to adopt an overall state (mood and attitude) that is similar to the child's mood and attitude. By gently imitating key behaviors and similar body movements; that is, by *finding ways to be alike*, we can easily establish rapport with a troubled, angry, or noncompliant child (Vaknin, 2008; O'Connor and Seymour, 2002). Some behaviors to imitate are:

- Matching breathing (rate and depth) to breathe in unison

- Mirroring gestures like hand and foot movements

- Matching voice (blending and harmonizing), i.e., speed, volume, or rhythm

- Mirroring the general style of movement; for example, how fast, how much gesturing, and how open or closed (e.g., arms and/or legs crossed)

- Matching the head tilt

- Mirroring the child's posture, e.g., leaning forward, straight up, or leaning back

- Adopting the same basic stance or sitting position; for example, resting on the same arm (your right to the child's left) to get a similar alignment and the same distribution of body weight

- Exchange matches; that is, we use a different body part, but we match the rhythm; for example, making a motion such as finger tapping to match the rhythm of the child's breathing. We can match the child's breathing pattern by moving a leg or a hand up and down accordingly. Alternatively, we can match arm movements with hand movements, and body movements with head movements

Persuasion Technique 25: Use Mirroring with Exchanged Matching

With mirroring and exchanged matching, we are creating rapport, which is at the heart of influencing and persuading children. By gently mirroring and matching certain key behaviors, we are producing an emotional state similar to the child's emotional state, significantly increasing our chances to elicit responses; that is, to persuade the child.

1. *Mirroring* is the process of copying the child's body language (facial expression, gestures, breathing, posture, or movement) and voice (sounds, speed,

volume, or rhythm). We can execute our mirroring exactly at the same time or slightly delayed, but doing it in such a way that we do not give the appearance of copying the child. This is why it is recommended that we mirror only some key movements and at selected times; for example, if the child crosses his arms, we do the same; if the child frowns, we frown; if the child talks fast, we talk fast.

2. *Exchanged matching* is a form of mirroring. With this neuro-linguistic technique, we *synchronize* body language and/or voice without directly copying the child. For example, if the child crosses his arms, we cross our legs; if the child scratches his head, we rub one arm; if the child coughs, we clear our throat; if the child talks fast, we move fast; if the child is fidgety, we sway our body. We can also use a different body part to match rhythm; for example, we can match a fast breathing pattern by moving one leg accordingly.

Persuasion Technique 26:
Use Matched Vocabulary or
Matched Speech

According to Mahony (2003), we increase rapport and mutual understanding when we use the child's preferred representational system or language predicates (visual, auditory, and kinesthetic or tactile). In simpler words, we increase rapport when we "speak the child's language." Predicates are sensory-based words and phrases; that is, predicates are messages that directly link to our senses and emotions, not to our brain (reason and analysis). We are often unaware that the words and sentences we use are biased toward one preferred sensory representational system, and that we can communicate better with children by simply speaking to them using their own (not ours!) preferred sensory vocabulary. From Mahony (2003) and O'Connor and Seymour (2002) we adapted the following examples of sensory-based vocabulary:

Visual

- I *see* what you mean
- It is *clear* as a day to me

- It *appears* to me
- In my mind's *eye*
- In *view* of your actions or behavior
- The future *looks* bright
- Take a *look* at yourself
- Get this *clear*
- I am *looking* closely at this idea
- *Watch* your language!
- *Watch* my lips
- Let me *draw* you a picture

Auditory

- Turn a *deaf ear*
- *Rings* a bell
- Pay attention to what I am *saying*
- You just don't *listen*
- Do I have to *spell* it out for you?
- *Music* to my ears
- I *hear* you loud and clear
- To *tell* you the truth
- In other *words*
- Are we on the same *wavelength*?

- Let me *put it* another way
- *State* your case

Kinesthetic

- It *feels* to me that…
- You are a *pain* in the neck
- I *feel* it in my bones
- Don't *push* your luck
- *Hang* in there!
- *Hold* on a second
- Haven't you *grasped* it yet?
- Going to *pieces*
- It *feels* all wrong
- Let's *move* slowly
- I can't *put my finger* on it

An example of *mismatched speech* is:

❖ **Child:** I can *see* it in my mind. I know I'm going to fail the spelling test (visual predicate).

❖ **Parent:** *Hold on a second* (kinesthetic predicate). You studied *hard* (kinesthetic) and you know those spelling words.

Examples of *matched speech* are:

- ❖ **Child:** I just can't *grasp* what I have to do with this graph (kinesthetic predicate).
- ❖ **Teacher:** Oh, what do you *feel* is the problem (kinesthetic predicate)? (Mahony, 2003)
- ❖ **Child:** I'll curse if I *feel* like it (kinesthetic predicate)!
- ❖ **Counselor:** Don't *push* your luck. Cursing *stops* at this very moment (kinesthetic predicates).

Persuasion Technique 27: Pace and Lead

From the neuro-linguistic literature, we get the pacing and leading technique (Vaknin, 2008; Nitsche, 2006; O' Connor and Seymour, 2002). This technique consists of four steps: *mirroring* or matching the child's posture, gestures, word choice, voice, or breathing. We mirror the child to establish *rapport*, which is the second step. The third step is *pacing*; that is, moving along with the child for a while and at the same speed before we try the fourth and last step, *leading*, where we lead the child into the mental and/or emotional state that we want, so that the child is receptive to our persuading and we are better able to help. More specifically, in the *pacing step*, we bond with the child and cement rapport through mirroring; in the *leading step*, we shift our physiology and attitude so that the child shifts her physiology and attitude. Leading is not going to work without well-established rapport, so we need to take our time bridging and bonding at the pacing level before attempting to lead the child.

In pacing and leading, first we mirror selected gestures and key behavior to match how the child is feeling. Then, we gradually change the mirrored behavior (e.g., breath pace and body language) to a more positive and resourceful state, moving the child into this new state. Next, we provide three examples of how to shift an angry and agitated child into a more positive and calmer state using the pacing and leading technique.

1. Synchronize your rate of breathing to become faster and then gradually slow it down, so that the child's breathing becomes deeper and slower, a physiology aligned with calmness.

2. Mirror the child by frowning, crossing your arms, leaning backwards, and keeping your palms closed (closed body posture). Gradually, shift to an open and inviting posture; that is, relax your face, unfold your arms, lean forward, open your palms, and move closer to the child. In other words, with your own *body language*, gradually shift the child from a *closed body posture* to an *open body posture*.

3. Do a *mood matching* (Mahony, 2003), matching the energy the child puts into his anger. The author recommends that, at the beginning of this procedure, you display your "energy level" as high as the child's energy level, but not higher. However, you display your energy as a *positive emotion* such as high concern or high interest. Then, lead the child toward a calmer state by progressively shifting your energy level downwards; for example, displaying a quieter tone of voice and showing smaller and slower body movements.

Persuasion Technique 28: The Voice Regulation Technique

From Nitsche (2006) we get the *voice regulation technique*. Most of the time, teachers and parents feel obligated to talk more, faster, and louder to get children listen, and to get children do what we want them to do. However, we can get compliance faster, and with less stress (without yelling), by simply regulating or manipulating our voice volume; more specifically, by reducing our voice volume and talking slower. For instance, to quiet a loud, angry child, follow the next steps:

> **Step 1:** Your first words need to be louder than the child's words. This creates a surprise element, and the child will become still.

> **Step 2:** Speech pause. By pausing and being silent, we show the child what we expect from her.

> **Step 3:** Start whispering. This causes the child to become more attentive and to listen more closely.

Step 4: Continue speaking and move from whispering to using your regular voice.

With this technique, we use very few words, and we show the child the behavior that we want from her (*show, do not tell technique*). In the next examples, Nitsche (2006) adapted the same voice regulation technique for use with a noisy class:

1. If the class sees you as you come into the classroom, do not say a word. Freeze your posture and establish eye contact. Maintain this posture and resist the temptation of talking. You are leading the class to be silent by being silent yourself. If the class does not notice you, you need to use your voice or a loud noise to get students to see you. In this case, use the next alternative.

2. Hold your body straight and freeze your posture. Keep your feet parallel to one another and pointing forward, making sure that your weight is balanced evenly on both feet. Stretch out one hand in front of you and hold it parallel to the floor; the hand is also frozen. Say, "GOOD MORNING LADIES (voice

louder than the volume of the class) (speech pause) *and gentlemen* (almost whispering). We will <u>begin now</u>!" Start this last sentence still whispering and then, glide up to your normal voice volume.

Persuasion Technique 29: Use Discipline Anchors

An anchor is a stimulus that always elicits the same reaction. The reaction can be either an action (can be observed), or it can take the form of a change in a mental (attitude) or emotional (feeling) state. An anchor can be anything we want; for example, a freeze posture, holding up one arm and saying "stop," pointing at one ear to signal the child to listen, counting down from five to one, putting on a green hat to signal story time, or clapping. When we repeatedly and systematically give the same signal connected to an event, concept, or idea, the signal and the event become connected or anchored with one another. The anchor creates a state of *positive expectation* (e.g., putting on a green hat creates the expectation "It's story time!"), resulting in a change of inner state; for example, from restless to attentive. Anchors then are reflexes; that is, automatic reactions that we create without using words or using very few words; and the more we use a particular anchor, the faster children respond to that anchor (Nitsche, 2006). We know that we created an effective anchor when we see children responding the way we want without the use of words.

Persuasion Technique 30: Use Space Anchors

A technique that is equally powerful at school and at home is to set up several space anchors on different spots in one room (Nitsche, 2006), or in different rooms if the child is at home. When we step into one of these space anchors children know, without words, what is happening next. Nitsche recommends for teachers to set up the following space anchors (parents can adapt at home using fewer anchors):

1. *The Scolding Space.* Freeze your posture, walk to the spot, stand stiffly, and finally look at the offender without saying a single word.

2. *The Attention Anchor* is a spot where the teacher stands at the beginning of a lesson to get the class attention; for example, next to the classroom door. To gain attention during the lesson, you need to use a second attention spot; for example, in front and middle of the classroom.

3. *The Teaching Spot* is the place in the classroom where the teacher communicates facts. As you walk, slowly and dramatically, toward this spot, children will look upon and become more attentive.

4. *The Storytelling Spot.* Put on a green hat, or any other visual signal, and walk toward this spot. Once there, share your story or current event.

5. *The Silence Spot* is where you step to signal total silence.

6. *The Hot Tips Spot.* Make a big "X" with masking tape on the floor in front of the room. Explain to children that every time you step into this spot, you expect to see that they assume the *hot tips posture*; that is, leaning forward with their eyes wide opened and listening attentively. On the hot tips spot you

share only key information. Once children are in the hot tips posture, you dramatically whisper the hot tip.

7. *The Discipline Anchor* should be next to where you post the classroom rules. Each time you discipline the class or a particular child, stand inside this spot. Nitsche (2006) warns that we never stand on the discipline anchor while doing a different activity. In addition, when disciplining, you need to put down everything associated with teaching, like books or chalk, or with any other activity. It is also important that you breathe calmly. Inside this anchor, say no more than one sentence or phrase; for example, a simple command like "You need to _____." Then, step out of the discipline anchor and continue teaching or interacting with the child as if nothing had happened. Outside the discipline anchor, make sure that your posture is relaxed, and that you are breathing fluidly; also, smile to the offender to signal to the child, "I discipline your behavior but I like you as a person." As Nitsche says, "A smile is the shortest distance between two people" (p. 175).

It is important to keep each anchor "clean" from one another. For example, if we have a homework anchor, we always use the exact same spot to deliver homework, not using the homework spot for any other activity. Alternatively, if we use a green hat to signal story time, we do not use the same hat to signal, "Get on line." Another way we can contaminate an anchor is when we send incongruent signals to children; for example, we are already standing inside the silence spot but we keep talking, or we gesture the "lower your voices" signal (hand palm down and lowered by degrees), but we raise our voice and yell. If we use them correctly; that is, systematically and "clean," anchors can become a powerful persuasive technique.

Persuasion Technique 31: Get a Commitment from the Child

Children are more likely to modify behavior if they give their word and commit themselves, so, after making your request always close it by asking, "Will you do it?"

Concluding Comments

The language patterns or messages we use define us and define the way we relate with children. Modifying what we say and the way we say it can do wonders in the way children behave. *Self-confidence* is key in persuasive discipline; when we feel confident that we can influence and persuade children, we project and spread that confidence. When disciplining children, be certain in everything you say and do. Talk with confidence and conviction; show confidence in your actions too. Believe in your ability to positively influence and persuade. The persuasive language patterns and ways of talking presented in this psycho-educational guide not only influence children toward positive behavior, but also help improving the overall atmosphere between the child and the adult. Persuasive language is behavioral language; when we command persuasive language, we promote positive behavior.

References

Mahony, T. (2003). *Words work! How to change your language to improve behaviour in your classroom.* Carmarthen, Wales: Crown House.

Nitsche, P. (2006). *Talk less. Teach more! Nonverbal classroom management. Group strategies that work.* Butler, PA: Pearls of Learning Press.

O' Connor, J., & Seymour, J. (2002). *Introducing NLP: Psychological skills for understanding and influencing people.* Hammersmith, London: Harper Element.

Schaefer, C. E. (1994). *How to influence children: A handbook of practical child guidance skills.* (Second Edition). Northvale, NJ: Jason Aronson.

Shapiro, L. E. (1994). *Tricks of the trade: 101 psychological techniques to help children grow and change.* King of Prussia, PA: Center for Applied Psychology.

Vaknin, S. (2008). *The big book of NLP techniques: 200+ patterns. Methods and strategies of neuro linguistic programming:* www.booksurge.com

Walker, H. M., & Walker, J. E. (1991). *Coping with noncompliance in the classroom: A positive approach for teachers.* Austin, Texas: Pro-Ed.

About the Author

Carmen Y. Reyes, *The Psycho-Educational Teacher*, has more than twenty years of experience as a self-contained special education teacher, resource room teacher, and educational diagnostician. In the classroom, Carmen has taught at all grade levels, from kindergarten to post-secondary. Carmen is an expert in the application of behavior management strategies, and in teaching students with learning or behavior problems. Her classroom background, in New York City and her native Puerto Rico, includes ten years teaching emotionally disturbed/behaviorally disordered children and four years teaching students with a learning disability or low cognitive functioning. Carmen has a bachelor's degree in psychology (University of Puerto Rico) and a master's degree in special education with a specialization in emotional disorders (Long Island University, Brooklyn: NY). She also has extensive graduate training in psychology (30+ credits). Currently, Carmen is a full-time writer. In her articles and books, she focuses in assessing children's learning capacities, alternative teaching procedures for low achieving students, and child guidance techniques and interventions.

Discover Other Titles by this Author

Watch Your Language! Ways of Talking and Interacting with Students that Crack the Behavior Code

All Behavior Is Communication: How To Give Feedback, Criticism, And Corrections That Improve Behavior

Thinking, Feeling, and Behaving: A Cognitive-Emotive Model to Get Children to Control their Behavior

School Help: A Teacher and Tutor Guide to Help the Older Student with Limited Word Reading Fluency

Keys To Meaning: What Teachers And Tutors Can Do To Improve Reading Comprehension Skills

*Keeping The Peace: Managing Students in Conflict
Using the Social Problem-Solving Approach*

*Essentials Of Emotional Communication For Reaching
The Unreachable Student: Where Do I Start? What Do I
Say? How Do I Do It?*

Connect with the Author Online

Blog

http://thepsychoeducationalteacher.blogspot.com/

Twitter

http://twitter.com/psychoeducation

Facebook

http://www.facebook.com/pages/The-Psycho-Educational-Teacher/168256836524091

Email

thepsychoeducationalteacher@gmail.com

37802763R00039

Made in the USA
San Bernardino, CA
25 August 2016